Let's DeCree

Let's DeCree

A 30-day Decree
Devotional for Children

OLa BekeS

My name is —————————————————————

I am ————— years old

My hobbies are —————————————————

—————————————————————————

This is My
Declaration Devotional

connect with Ola Bekes
olabekes90@gmail.com

Designed & typeset by **Elaion Media**
Instagram: @elaionmedia
Illustrated with assets from
freepik.com

Dedication

First and foremost, I want to thank God for the sustainability, inspiration and zeal required to successfully complete this project. Your grace is more than enough for me.

I dedicate this work to Kolawole Bekes, my devoted husband. I appreciate you joining me on this path and sharing this epiphany with me. Beyond what words can express, I love you. I also dedicate this book to my devoted kids, who gave birth to a new version of me and whom God used to reveal my calling. Royal, Royce, and Royelle. In my heart, you have a special place. And you have my utmost affection.

I dedicate this book to my parents, Mr. Adeyinka and Mrs. Funmilola Balogun, whom I will always love. I appreciate you for instructing me in the path of the Lord, giving me clear instructions, and helping me establish a strong foundation. I want you to know that I will always do my best to make you proud.

Contents

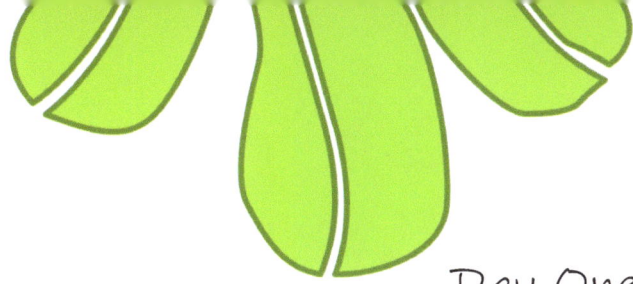

Born to Exhude Joy

"For this Day is holy to our Lord. Do not sorrow for the Joy of the Lord is your strength."
Nehemiah 8:10b

This is the day the Lord has made, I shall rejoice and be glad. Lord, I will only have joy in my heart, laughter in my mouth, and speed under my feet as I start today. I am filled with the pleasure of the Lord, and his promises are always fulfilled in my life. Being in a state of joy makes me stronger from the inside out. Everyone in my immediate vicinity is affected by my happiness and smiles. In the name of Jesus, I have declared. Amen.

Born to Live in Faith

"God has not given me the spirit of fear but of power, love and of a sound mind"
1 Timothy 1:7

Therefore, I declare in the name of Jesus that I have a renewed mind, a sound mind, an excellent spirit, fear has no power over me because I am filled with hope and trust in the fact that God has my back, I declare that I display faith rather than fear, and I am brave in the face of hardship. I naturally have a clear mind full of possibilities, and my love for the kingdom of God is ignited so that I can withstand all the enemy's darts. In the name of Jesus, I command that these things be carried out. Amen.

Born to be Peaceful

"Do not be anxious about anything. Instead, in every situation with prayer and petition with thanksgiving, tell your requests to God. And the peace that surpasses all understanding will guard your hearts and minds in Christ Jesus."
Philippians 4:6

Father, you created me in your image, full of love, peace, and joy. So, Lord, I decree that in every situation in which I find myself, I will maintain peace; even when life tries to shake my focus and stability in you, I will remain steadfast; help me not to shake; and let the peace instilled in me overshadow the fear of the world. Help me to remember that you are always listening in any situation and keep my heart full of gratitude knowing you have my back. In Jesus name I receive these as done. Amen.

Born with a Receptive Spirit

"My son, give attention to my words; Incline your ear to my sayings"
Proverbs 4:20

Father, I decree and declare that the power of the Holy Spirit is powerful on me. I pay attention to God's instruction, let the spirit of responsibility come upon me, let the spirit of laziness and entitlement have no place in my life, help me to hide myself in you, feel my dreams with instructions that will navigate my steps in life, open my eyes to the mysteries of heaven and my life, feel my heart with your word whenever I am afraid, help me to trust in you, the mouths of my parents will be filled with testimony because of me. These are my decrees, and I receive them in Jesus name. Amen.

Born to be Fruitful

"Even so, every good tree bears good fruit, but a bad tree bears bad fruit. A good tree cannot bear bad fruit, nor can a bad tree bear good fruit."
Matthew 7:17-18

Father, I pray that I will bear good fruit from the goodness that is within me, that I will be known for the good that I do, and that I will express the fruits of trustworthiness, self-control, confidence, honesty, and humility in everything I do. Lord, keep me safe from the fowler's trap; let my good fruits be so obvious that they disrupt the enemy's plans. Lord, lead me, guide me, and be my refuge; let my light shine before men so that they may see my good works and glorify you. Amen.

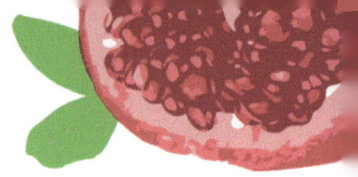

Confessions on the Fruit of the Spirit

"But the fruit of the Spirit is love, joy, peace, patience, kindness, goodness, faithfulness, gentleness, self-control; against such things there is no law."
Galatians 5:22-23

Love
(John 15:12)
I Love the Lord with all my Heart.

Joy
(Nehemiah 8:10)
The Joy of the Lord is my strength.

Peace
(Philippians 4:7)
I have the peace of God that surpasses all understanding.

Patience
(2 Corinthians 6:)
I Exercise Patience and a Calm spirit.

Kindness
(Romans 11:22)
I am Kind to everyone I come across with.

Goodness
(Psalm 107:9)
The Goodness of the Lord finds expression in my heart.

Faithfulness
(Hebrews 11:1)
My heart is full of faith and I trust God with all my heart.

Gentleness
(James 3:17)
I am gentle in my actions and dealings with those around me.

Self control
(2 Timothy 1:7)
I Love the Lord with all my Heart.

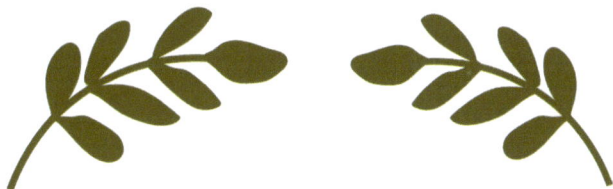

My Prayer Request

Heavenly Father, _____

_____

_____

_____

_____

_____

_____

_____

Born a Beautiful Creation

"I will praise You, for I am fearfully and wonderfully made; marvelous are Your works, and that my soul knows very well."
Psalm 139:14

Father, I appreciate you for making me in your unique image. I love my body, I love who I am exactly as I am, and I love being the boy or girl that God made me to be. Because God took his time creating me, I am content with my abilities, talents, and beauty. When God saw me, He said 'what He has created is marvelous in His sight'. I am assured in the person God has made me to be, disciplined with my body, and determined to treat it with respect. No one will steal my innocence, and I won't experience sexual assault, or molestation. God's angels are continuously watching out for me and defending me. I'm safeguarded and safe. These are my decrees and I receive it. Amen.

Born into Sonship

"For this Day is holy to our Lord. Do not sorrow for the Joy of the Lord is your strength."
Nehemiah 8:10b

Thank you, Jesus, for coming to the point of death for me and for giving me back my sonship. Lord, I confess that I repent of all my sins in my thoughts, deeds, and feelings. I am a child of God, and I am no longer a slave to sin. I express the fullness of life in Christ Jesus, I am forgiven, I am free, sin has no power over me, and I am alive in Christ because I have been purchased at a price. Let mercy always speak for me instead of judgement. Thank you, father, for these are declarations and I receive them done in Jesus' name. Amen.

Born into Grace

"And God is able to make all grace abound toward you, that you, always having all sufficiency in all things, may have an abundance for every good work."
2 Corinthians 9:8

I enjoy the grace that allows me access to your throne of mercy, favor surrounds me like a shield, and I receive the grace of provision that I always have everything I need, that I will never go without anything good, and that God will generously provide for my parents so that we have enough and can share with others. Father, I ask this in the name of Jesus. I enjoy the grace for ease, I also enjoy the grace for speed. In the name of Jesus, I receive these. Amen.

Born to be Fearless

"God has not given me the spirit of fear but of power, love and of a sound mind"
1 Timothy 1:7

Father, I thank you for being my source and supply today. Thank you for enabling me to breathe. Thank you, Lord, for the assurance I have in you, for bearing me and guiding me in the right direction, and for holding my hand since only you know what the future has for me. Thank you, Lord, for your assistance, for ensuring that I won't be left behind in life, and for providing comfort by putting out your hand to me. These are my declarations; they are mine in Jesus' name. Amen.

Born for Such a Time as This

"You are the salt of the earth. But if the salt loses its saltiness, how can it be made salty again? It is no longer good for anything, except to be thrown out and trampled underfoot."
Matthew 5:13

(Insert your name) was born for this time, to be a solution to my generation, a pace setter, a masterpiece for Jehovah, building a generation with a kingdom mindset, I am distinguished with excellence, I have the wisdom to locate hidden riches in secret places, kings are coming to the brightness of my rising, the wealth of gentiles are my heritage, Royalty is my identity. These are my decrees, and I command them to be carried out in Jesus' name. Amen.

Born into Royalty

"You shall also be a crown of glory, In the hand of the LORD, And a royal diadem in the hand of your God."
Isaiah 62:3

Thank you, Lord, because I come from a royal lineage, and there is a king in me; thank you, Lord, because I am a splendor of beauty, and a signet of royalty. The enemy will never steal my glory, no one will ever hide my radiance, no scheme of man or power in hell will ever be able to take me away from his promises, because I am a king who rules, reigns, and dominates. In Jesus' name, I receive these done. Amen.

Activity

Declare God's Promises

I know who I am

I'm no longer a slave to sin

I'm the righteousness of God

I know what to do

I'm free

I'm a child of God

I have the Spirit of God

I'm bold

My Prayer Request

Heavenly Father, ——————————————————

———————————————————————————

———————————————————————————

———————————————————————————

———————————————————————————

———————————————————————————

———————————————————————————

———————————————————————————

Born into Overflow

"As He showers you with uncommon favor, you will walk in the reality of His overflow. He can do exceedingly, abundantly above all that we ask or think. He is the God of the overflow."
Ephesians 3:20

Thank you, Father, for allowing me to live an abundant life. Father, please help me not to let others stop my flow; the mistakes of my parents or generation before me will not stop my flow; I am connected to the right people who will influence me to overflow in all aspects spiritually, mentally, physically, emotionally, and academically; and please allow an overflow of your sweetness and loving kindnesses in my life. These are my decrees, and I command them to be carried out in Jesus' name. Amen.

Born into Possibilities

"I can do all things through Christ who strengthens me."
Philippians 4:13

Thank you Father, for giving me strength. I am so excited about my future and what God has planned for me. He has given me strength and wisdom. I am qualified, energetic, and full of potential. I am an innovator, an inventor, extremely creative, skillful, and full of God-given ideas that have the power to change the course of the universe. God is putting dreams in my heart, and I'm living them fully. In the name of Jesus, I have declared. Amen.

Born into Greatness

"You shall increase my greatness, And comfort me on every side."
Psalm 71:21

I am greatly increased intellectually, my reasoning is greatly enhanced, my heart is alert, my mind is receptive, my cognitive skills are sharp, my learning capabilities are top notch, my lips are anointed, my sleep is blessed, my dreams are filled with divine revelations, I am a forward thinker, and in my chosen field I blossom. Father, thank you for bestowing such greatness upon me. In the name of Jesus, I have declared. Amen.

Born into Provision

"God will supply all my needs according to his riches in glory"
Philippians 4:19

Father, thank you for making provisions in advance so that I won't be without anything. Lord, grant me the grace to hold onto my purpose and to tap into its richness. No one will be able to fulfil my destiny in instead of me; I will not be replaced. I have all the knowledge and tools necessary to do everything for which God created me. I also receive support from all directions in order to fulfill the responsibility that God has given me. In the name of Jesus, I decree that these things be carried out. Amen.

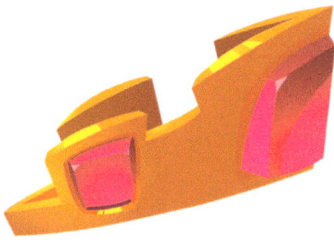

Born into Wealth

"You shall remember the LORD your God, for it is he who gives you power to get wealth, that he may confirm his covenant that he swore to your fathers, as it is this day You shall remember the Lord your God, for it is he who gives you power to get wealth, that he may confirm his covenant that he swore to your fathers, as it is this day."
Deuteronomy 8:18

Father in Jesus name, I decree that I am breaking out of every generational curses of poverty, poor mindset, I break from a circle of negativity, and I am embracing generational blessings that says you will bless me and multiply me, you will also bless whatsoever is found in my hands, the Lord will increase my offspring, I will partake of the blessings of the land, I will eat the honey of every land I step my feet, I enjoy the grace that enables me to create wealth. These are my decrees and I receive them done in Jesus' name. Amen.

Born to Flourish

"The righteous will flourish like a palm tree and grow like a cedar in Lebanon: planted in the house of the LORD, they will flourish in the courts of our God."
Psalm 92:12-13

Dear Lord, in all my ways I acknowledge God, I am the righteousness of God in Christ Jesus, goodness and mercy pursue me throughout my life, nothing dies or diminishes in my hands, I grow from strength to strength, whatever I lay my hands on prospers, I smell like myrrh, and I am anointed to prosper. I declare that I will dwell in the house of the Lord all the days of my life. In the name of Jesus, I have declared. Amen.

Born to be a Blessing

"The Lord blesses you and keep you; the Lord make his face shine on you and be gracious to you; the Lord turn his face toward you and give you peace.
Numbers 6:24-26

Father, I pray that you continue to shower me with benefits as I mature. Instead of running out of them, may there be an overflow. My brightness draws the wealth of nations, I take part in the sweetness of the country, the blessing of the Lord creates room for me and adds no sadness, I enjoy God's favor and his mercy, may your blessing follow me wherever I go, may the collaborate with me. These are my decrees and I receive them done in Jesus name. Amen.

Activity

42

My Prayer Request

Heavenly Father, ———————————————————

———————————————————————————

———————————————————————————

———————————————————————————

———————————————————————————

———————————————————————————

———————————————————————————

Born to Add Value

"You are the salt of the earth. But if the salt loses its saltiness, how can it be made salty again? It is no longer good for anything, except to be thrown out and trampled underfoot."
Matthew 5:13

Lord, you made me to enhance flavor to the world; I was made to sweeten the world. Father, may I never lose my flavor. Lord, may I never lose my saltiness. That wonder you have placed inside of me; may I never lose it. Father, may I ever be a source of inspiration to those around me. Lord, may I never be a castaway. May my presence on this planet matter. I command these things to be carried out in the name of Jesus. Amen.

Born to Honour

"Honor your father and your mother, that your days may be long upon the land which the LORD your God is giving you."
Exodus 20:12

Father, please give me a submissive heart. Lord, teach me to honor my parents. Grant me a willing heart, Lord, and the desire to listen more and speak less. Help me to be teachable. Father, grant me the wisdom to use the guidance provided to me as I navigate my future. Let the benefits of honoring my parents descend upon me and provide me a long life. Persons are allowed to bless me because of the honor I've given to my parents and other important people in my life. I'll excel in this. In Jesus name I have declared. Amen.

Born to be Focused

"But they will never follow a stranger; in fact, they will run away from him because they do not recognize a stranger's voice."
John 10:5

Father, come into our universities, preschools, high schools, and all the staff members there with your power. Give them your wisdom and grace. Lord, may I not become lost as a student, may I attract the right friends, may I not be distracted, and may I not lose myself to the world as I listen to the voice of the Holy Spirit. I don't recognize the voices of strangers. My encounters, revelations, and purpose will become more powerful as I grow in stature and wisdom, and the enemy will be unable to destroy what you have in store for me. These are my declarations, and I am seeing results. In Jesus name. Amen.

Activity

S **Self discipline:** I Express self discipline today.

C **Confidence:** Today I am extremely confident.

H **Holy Spirit:** The Holy Spirit is my comforter always

O **Outstanding:** I stand out today

O **Overcome Temptation:** Today I overcome any temptation that comes my way

L **Light:** I am light and my path shines ever brighter

My Prayer Request

Heavenly Father, ————————————————————

————————————————————————————

————————————————————————————

————————————————————————————

————————————————————————————

————————————————————————————

————————————————————————————

————————————————————————————

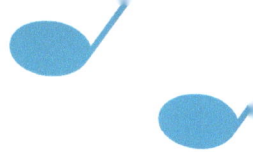

Born into Gladness

*"You love righteousness and hate wickedness;
Therefore God, your God, has anointed you with the
oil of gladness more than your companions."*
Psalm 45:7

Thank you, Lord, for anointing me with joy. I now have access to a wealth of resources because of the oil of joy you placed on me. I now have the honor and royal anointing you bestowed upon me. I am anointed with excellence, I experience ease, and the oil of gladness on my head attracts the ideal person who will lead me to purpose. Since I am the head and not the tail, I am protected from evil. May my cup overflow as he anoints my head with a fresh anointing, in Jesus' name I receive. Amen.

Born to Trust God

"Trust in the LORD with all your heart. And lean not on your own understanding; in all your ways acknowledge Him, And He will make your paths straight."
Proverbs 3: 5-6

Father, grant me the wisdom to understand that without you, I am nothing. I choose to rely on the wisdom from above to guide my decisions. Please direct me in the right direction. Let the knowledge of you guide my understandings and actions. In everything I do, Lord, I acknowledge you as my source and enabler for the rest of my life. I mandate that these things be carried out in the name of Jesus. Amen.

Declare God's Promises

T My thumb reminds me to Trust God Always

P My pointy finger reminds me to pray for others

I My index finger reminds that I am who I am in Christ Jesus

R My Ring finger reminds to Recognize God's blessing always

P My pinky fingers remind me that I am not perfect, but He loves me

My Prayer Request

Heavenly Father, ——————————————

_____

_____

_____

_____

_____

_____

Born to Shine

"You are the light of the world. A town built on a hill cannot be hidden."
Matthew 5:14

I was created to be noticed, to demonstrate my good deeds, and to bring honor to my father. For these reasons, the enemy will not bury my shine, life will not hide my light, nothing will steal my spotlight, and my brilliance will not be buried. I will not ignore my calling or make stupid mistakes that will prevent me from leaving my imprint on this planet. I SHINE SO BRIGHTLY THAT EVEN DARKNESS CAN'T SEE ME. I command that these things be done in Jesus' name. Amen.

Memory Verses

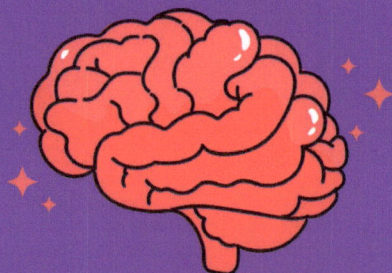

- *"Let the word of Christ dwell in you richly."*
  Colossians 3:16

- *"Whoever will call on the name of the Lord will be saved."*
  Romans 10:13

- *"Children, obey your parents in the Lord, for this is right."*
  Ephesians 6:1

- *"Be kind and compassionate to one another, forgiving each other."*
  Ephesians4: 32

- *"Whoever will call on the name of the Lord will be saved."*
  Romans 10:13

My Prayer Request

Heavenly Father, _____

_____

_____

_____

_____

_____

_____

Born to Have an Expected End

"For I know the thoughts that I think toward you, says the LORD, thoughts of peace and not of evil, to give you a future and a hope."
Jeremiah 29:11

God has already planned a wonderful future for me, one that is filled with miracles, serenity, and joy. I won't let the conditions around me know how I feel, and I won't let my past ruin my future. Because of his blessings, prosperity, and mind-blowing thoughts for me, I choose to be optimistic about everything that is happening around me. In the name of Jesus, I command that these things be carried out. Amen.

Born with a Mantle

" In the last days, God says, I will pour out my Spirit on all people; your sons and daughters will prophesy, your young men will see visions, your old men will dream dreams."
Acts 2:17

Thank you, Jesus, for the outpouring of your Spirit on me. Father, grant me the mantle of prayer and prophetic manifestation so that I may be delivered from the spirit of negligence. My zeal for Christ will not be shaken or under attack by the spirit of error, false dreams and lying visions. Harmful influences will not weaken my zeal for Christ, I begin to explore the prophetic, healing mantles rest upon my destiny, and God will begin to give me instructions about my life. In the name of Jesus, I receive it! Amen.

Memory Verses

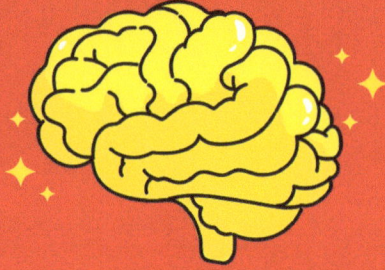

- *"When I am afraid, I will trust you."*
  Psalm 56:3

- *"I will give you thanks with my whole heart."*
  Psalm 138:1

- *"Your word is a lamp to my feet
  and a light to my path."*
  Psalm 119:105

- *"I am with you always."*
  Matthew 28:20

- *"Be kind to one another."*
  Ephesians 4:32

My Prayer Request

Heavenly Father, ————————————————

_____

_____

_____

_____

_____

_____

Born with the Breath of the Almighty

"Then the LORD God formed the man out of the dust of the ground and blew into his nostrils the breath of life, and the man became a living being."
Genesis 1:27

Father, thank you for breathing life into me from conception. May I never lose your breath in my life, breathe afresh into my lungs, your breath which gives me new essence, your breath that keeps me relevant, your breath makes me a world changer, and your breath makes me a light to my generation. Lord, breathe into me and resurrect everything in my life that appears to be dead. May the breath of life make me even more unique. Enable this to heal my heart and my body. These are my decrees, and I command that they be carried out in the name of Jesus. Amen.

God's Creation

"But it is the spirit in a person, the breath of the Almighty, that gives them understanding."
Job 32:8 (NIV)

"The Spirit of God has made me; the breath of the Almighty gives me life."
Job 33:4 (NIV)

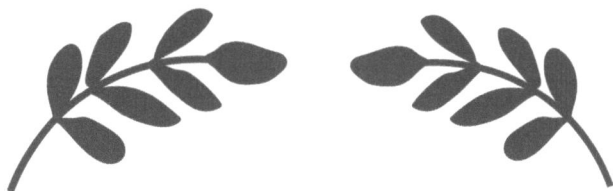

My Prayer Request

Heavenly Father, —————————————————————

———————————————————————————————

———————————————————————————————

———————————————————————————————

———————————————————————————————

———————————————————————————————

———————————————————————————————

one

two

three

Born to Discern

"But solid food is for the mature, who by constant use have trained themselves to distinguish good from evil."
Hebrews 5:14

Father, help me to exercise my senses as a child so that I can be spiritually alert and know the action behind every motive. Father, anoint my eyes to see what you have in store for me, anoint my ears to hear what you have in store for me, and anoint my understanding so that I can begin to comprehend your purpose for my life. I begin to discern the right company to keep, I am bold to say no to things that are not of God, and I will not be misled because I am capable of discernment. These are my declaration and I receive them done in Jesus' name. Amen.

Noah's Ark

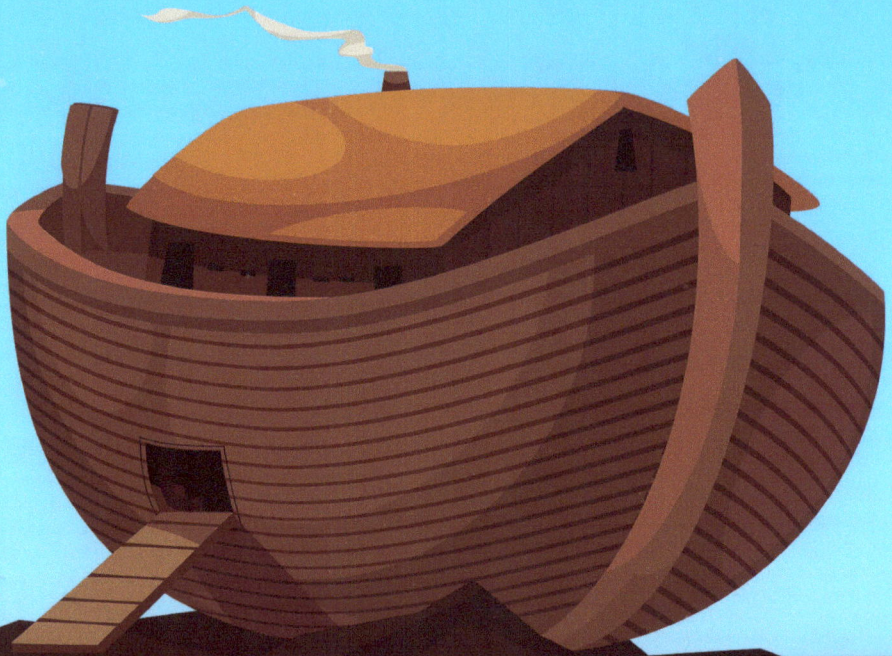

"But Noah found favor in the eyes of the Lord. This is the account of Noah and his family. Noah was a righteous man, blameless among the people of his time, and he walked faithfully with God."
Genesis 8-9 (NIV)

My Prayer Request

Heavenly Father, ———————————————————

———————————————————————————

———————————————————————————

———————————————————————————

———————————————————————————

———————————————————————————

———————————————————————————

———————————————————————————

Born into Divine Access

"There is a way that seems right to a man, but its end is the way of death."
Proverbs 16:35

Father, help me to follow the path you have outlined for me, guide me in the correct direction, and assist me in controlling my emotions. Father destroys every flaw in my body that prevents me from accessing spiritual things, giving me the grace to subdue my flesh as I follow God's word. Lord, make my flesh dead to sin so that it has no power over me. May I stay focused on the correct path and avoid taking the wrong path, and may I make heaven proud. In Jesus name I Receive. Amen

Jacob becomes Israel

"Then the man said, 'let me go for it is daybreak.;
But Jacob replied, 'I will no let you go until you bless
me.' Then the man asked him, 'What is your name?'
'Jacob' he answered. Then the man said, 'Your name
will no longer be Jacob, but Israel, because you
have struggled with God and with humans and have
overcome."
Genesis 32:26-28 (NIV)

My Prayer Request

Heavenly Father, ——————————————————

——————————————————————————

——————————————————————————

——————————————————————————

——————————————————————————

——————————————————————————

——————————————————————————

——————————————————————————

Born to Walk in the Way of the Righteous

"Blessed is the man Who walks not in the counsel of the ungodly, nor stands in the path of sinners, nor sits in the seat of the scornful; But his delight is in the law of the LORD, And in His law, he meditates day and night."
Psalm 1:1-2

Father Lord, help me to let my heart be drawn to your will and ways. As I read your word, help me to meditate on it. I will walk by your word day and night. Help me Lord that I will not succumb to peer pressure. Help me rise above false societal beliefs. Help me stand strong as a child of God in these times. I won't forget your instructions and laws you have placed in my heart. In Jesus name I receive it done. Amen.

Enoch's Walk

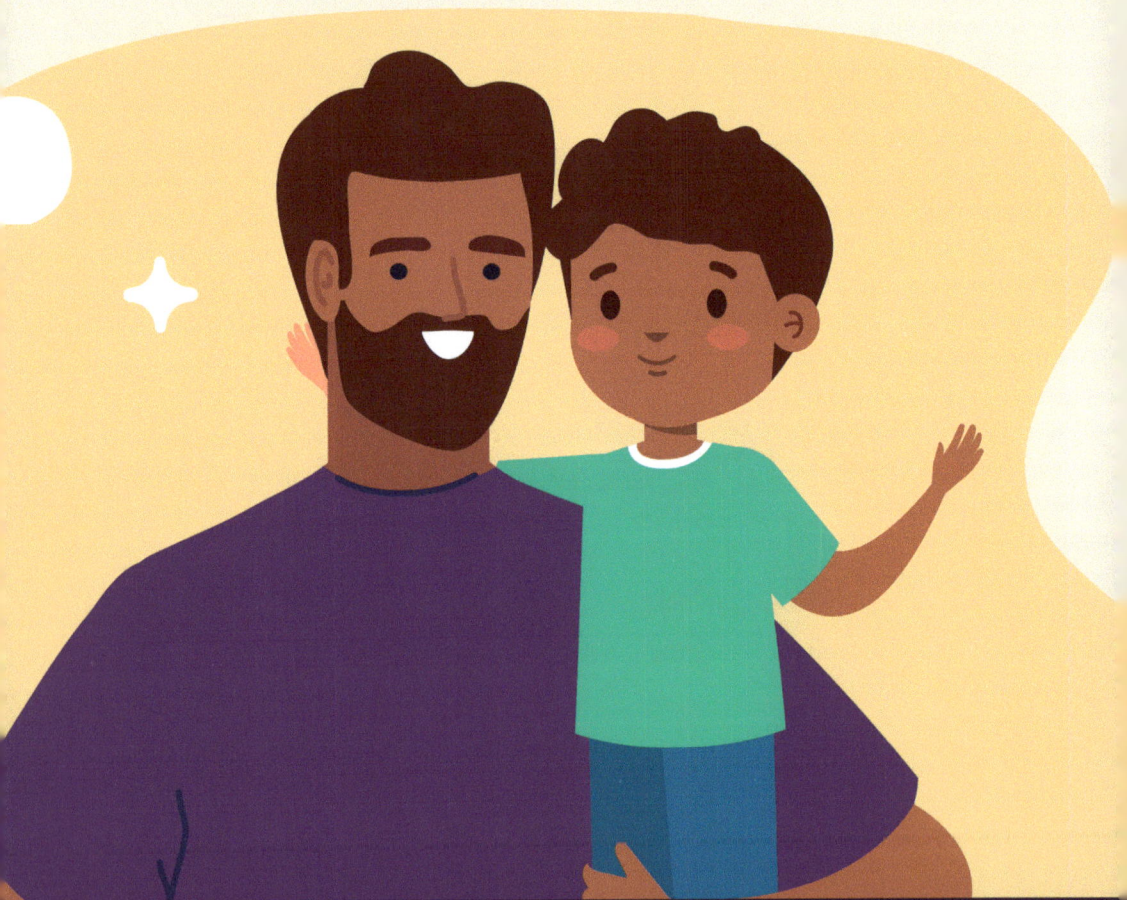

"Enoch walked faithfully with God; then he was no more, because God took him away."
Genesis 5:24 (NIV)

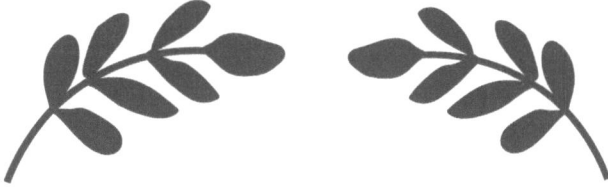

My Prayer Request

Heavenly Father, —————————————————————

—————————————————————————————

—————————————————————————————

—————————————————————————————

—————————————————————————————

—————————————————————————————

—————————————————————————————